THE HISTORY TREE SERIES

The History Tree Series books are designed for little people to learn history in a fun way, to appreciate old growth trees, and to interact with their grown-up reader for enriched content. Each page has easy to read words and concepts for the children, plus additional content for the adult reader (labeled as READER GUIDANCE) to add to the story as they see fit. Some historical stories have sad or violent elements. It will be up to the adult to choose how much to share, and at what age. Enjoy and get out and see some of these trees in person, they are all in existence today.

Your "patriarch" might be called Grandpa, Abuelo, or Papi.

If this ancient tree could talk,
what would its story be?

The Patriarch's tale goes back a long, long time because our storyteller is a Limber Pine.

Reader Guidance: The Old Patriarch Tree is a Pinus flexilis. They are very long lived. This particular tree is estimated to be 1100 years old and the oldest tree in Grand Teton National Park. Limber Pines are solitary, highland pines, that can twist and turn but rarely splinter, even in ferocious winds and storms. The Old Patriarch Tree is bowed and bent, with half of its trunk missing due to lightning strikes and fire scars. The "Old Patriarch Tree" sits majestically in the sagebrush flats framed by the snowcapped Cathedral Group of the Tetons.

As time passed, our limber pine felt that change would come soon. It began when he met a lone white man walking with snow shoes.

This man's name was John Colter.
He was a rugged explorer and guide.

His job was to wade raging rivers and climb mountain rises. He discovered rare and unusual things like steaming geysers!

Reader Guidance: In 1803, Colter enlisted in the Lewis and Clark Expedition as a hunter/scout. When the expedition returned to St. Louis, in 1806, they were met by two trappers named Hancock and Dickson. They were headed to the Yellowstone River, and Colter was not ready to return to "civilization." Colter was granted a discharge to join them, and the trio began the journey in August, 1806.

When Colter went home, no one believed he saw these things. Yellow stones and spouting steam? Perhaps he just had a super strange dream!

Reader guidance: Though his exact route isn't known, it is certain that Colter traveled alone with only his rifle and pack, covering an estimated 500 miles. During the winter of 1807, with the help of Indian guides, he was thought to have crossed the Wind River Mountains, the Teton Range, and was probably the first white man to see Jackson Hole and The Grand Canyon of the Yellowstone. On his return to Fort Raymond in the spring of 1808, he described the thermal wonders of Yellowstone. Most were skeptical of his descriptions and Yellowstone soon became known as "Colter's Hell."

The Patriarch said goodbye to brave John Colter, but was soon visited by mountain men called "trappers," some even tougher and bolder.

Reader Guidance: For the mountain men, a "hole" indicated a high valley that was surrounded by mountains. As others followed Colter's example, Jackson's Hole (the valley near The Old Patriarch Tree) became one of the prime areas of interest. Most of the famous mountain men that trapped in the West in the early 1800's traveled the trails that crossed the area: Jim Bridger, Jedediah Smith, William Sublette, and David Jackson were among them.

They told The Patriarch they wanted to find fur.
The soft, fuzzy beaver was what they preferred.

People liked tall beaver hats and warm beaver coats, so the trappers sent fur back on big riverboats.

For the Patriarch, more winters came and went. Through his valley new humans travelled, feeling like they were sent.

Reader Guidance: A philosophy that was given the name "Manifest Destiny" in 1845, pushed forward the 19th-century U.S. territorial expansion. Manifest Destiny held that the United States was destined by God to subdue native people and spread Christianity and capitalism across the continent.

Moms, dads, and children walked and walked. Their big cart wheels left grooves in the rocks.

Reader Guidance: The pioneer legacy left its mark not far from our History Tree. Carved into the stony hills, The Oregon Trail was one of the primary routes used by emigrants heading westward across the American continent in the 1840s. Many remnants of the trek are still visible but Oregon Trail tracks are most notable because they were cut into solid rock.

A few pioneers stayed on, but most continued to roll. The Patriarch welcomed newcomers that named his valley "Jackson's Hole."

Reader Guidance: Members of The Church of Jesus Christ of Latter-day Saints, then called Mormons, settled east of Blacktail Butte near the turn of the 19-century. These settlers first arrived in the 1890s from Idaho establishing a community (named Grovont by the U.S. Post Office) known today as "Mormon Row." Homesteaders established 27 homesteads in the Grovont area because of fertile soil, shelter from winds by Blacktail Butte and access to the Gros Ventre River. Despite the harsh conditions of Jackson Hole, Mormon settlers grew crops by using irrigation. These hardy settlers dug ditches by hand and with teams of horses, building an intricate network of levees and dikes to funnel water from central ditches to their fields between 1896 and 1937. Water still flows in some of these ditches today.

Now, rugged men on horses rested in the shade of The Patriarch's branches.

Our famous storyteller tree now had new tales to tell of cowboys and cattle ranches.

Reader Guidance: Josiah David Ferrin, nicknamed "Uncle Si," was the closest thing Jackson Hole came to having a cattle baron. He ranched near the town of Jackson, WY until 1908 when President Roosevelt opened lands in the Buffalo Valley to homesteaders. Ferrin purchased surrounding properties and was awarded a lucrative contract to supply beef to Bureau of Reclamation Service crews building Jackson Lake Dam. By 1920, Ferrin's family owned the largest ranch in Jackson Hole with 2,000 cattle on 400 acres - a "kingdom" that earned him the nickname "Cattle King of Wyoming." Today, the grasslands near The Old Patriarch Tree remind us that herds of cattle once roamed the area.

Tourists and Naturalists came next.

The tree learned that visitors wanted to study forest creatures- from grizzly bears to tiny insects.

Readers Guidance: The conservation effort in Jackson Hole began more than 100 years ago. The harsh winter of 1908-1909 resulted in a large die-off of elk leading to the creation of the national Elk Refuge. More than 50 years ago the Murie families hosted like-minded conservationists who drafted language for the Wilderness Act of 1964. Other organizations protect wildlife and resources, educate the next generation of park supporters and conservationists, and national park history enthusiasts preserve the tales and artifacts that have shaped the Grand Teton that visitors know today.

Conservation is a big word that means to take care of and protect.

One-thousand-year-old
trees need conservation, too. So take care of special trees like The Patriarch because...

if they could talk, their stories would ROCK!!

Reader Guidance: To find The Old Patriarch, you're looking for a limber pine standing alone in the sage brush flats. The Teton Park Road (sometimes called the Inner Park Road) used to go past the tree, but it's now 3/4 mile to hike to get to it. The road now sweeps farther to the west and closer to String Lake. Sagebrush now grows where the old road bed once was.

ABOUT THE AUTHOR

Tana Holmes was born in Colorado and raised in the mountains and windswept plains of Wyoming. Her early years spent in the shadow of the Tetons and roaming Yellowstone and Shoshone National Forest formed her love of history and nature. Archaeological digs and river-chilled watermelon every weekend were a great way to grow up! As an adult, Tana is an award-winning thirty-year professional public school educator, a mom, and still a nature lover.

Authorship of The History Tree Series started as a concept introduced by her daughter, Tori, while walking the battlefield at San Jacinto, Texas. They brainstormed that a talking tree as an eyewitness to history-making events was a great way to engage children in learning and loving their heritage. Her debut History Tree was Alamo Tree. Now as more volumes in the series release, Tana anticipates an opportunity to reach children globally with their own local "celebritree" story teller. Visit her and the History Trees at www.historytreeseries.com. If you liked The Old Patriarch Tree, please leave a review on Amazon.com.

ABOUT THE ILLUSTRATOR

Mahfuja Selim is a freelance illustrator mostly working on Children books for 8 years. She loves creating characters and locations that come from around the world. Her semi-cartoony drawing style sets her apart in the field. Her work has been published throughout the world in children's books, magazines, educational publications, children's games and packaging. She works with modern digital drawing tools at hand combined with all the traditional knowledge Children love her work!

www.ingramcontent.com/pod-product-compliance
Lightning Source LLC
Chambersburg PA
CBHW081238080526
44587CB00022B/3983